# What Mama Said

# *What Mama Said*

By Gladys Seedorf

Seedorf Book Publishing
Battle Creek, Michigan

*What Mama Said*
Published by Seedorf Book Publishing
11135 Burrows Road
Battle Creek, MI 49014
(269) 425-8747
g01131963@yahoo.com

Gladys Seedorf, Publisher
QualityPress.info, Production Coordinator
Printed Page, Interior and Cover Design

ALL RIGHTS RESERVED

No part of this book may be reproduced or transmitted in any form or by any means – electronic or mechanical, including photocopying, recording or by any information storage and retrieved system without written permission from the authors, except for the inclusion of brief quotations in a review.

Seedorf Books are available at special discounts for bulk purchases, sales promotions, fund raising or educational purposes.

Copyright © 2013 by Gladys Seedorf
ISBN #: 978-0-9892590-8-8
Library of Congress Control Number: 2013906245

# Dedication

I dedicate this book to my mother, Willie Jewel Peterson, who has always been a wonderful inspiration throughout my life. She has always been there for me while showing great wisdom, kindness and compassion. The valuable lessons that I've learned have served me well, and I've passed them on to my children.

*Gladys Seedorf*

# Acknowledgements

I would like to thank my dear and precious friends and neighbors, Dr. and Mrs. Roger Thomson, for giving me the idea and encouragement to write this book.

George and Jeannette Martin are very dear to my heart as well. Regardless of what I need they are always willing to provide assistance.

My dear friend, Karin DeGraw, thank you for standing by my side and providing many hours of assistance in bringing my ideas to fruition.

My family and I are truly exceedingly and abundantly blessed by the mere acquaintance of these people.

Last, but not least, I want to thank my husband, James, and my two daughters, Danielle and Monique, for providing the utmost support and encouragement during this process.

*Gladys Seedorf*

# Contents

| | |
|---|---|
| **Part One – Meet Mama** | 1 |
| Willie's Story | 3 |
| **Part Two – What Mama Said … And Why** | 11 |
| **Part Three – Mama's Favorite Songs & Scripture** | 71 |
| This Little Light of Mine | 72 |
| 99 ½ Won't Do | 73 |
| Travlin' Shoes | 74 |
| I Know it Was the Blood | 75 |
| I Don't Know What I Would Do Without the Lawd | 76 |
| Proverbs 31:10-31 | 77 |
| **Part Four – Mama's Favorite Recipes** | 79 |
| Baked Sweet Potatoes | 80 |
| Red Velvet Cake | 81 |
| Sweet Potato Pie | 83 |
| Sour Cream Pound Cake | 84 |
| Ice Box Rolls | 85 |
| Hummingbird Cake | 87 |
| **In Conclusion** | 89 |
| **About The Author** | 91 |

*Gladys Seedorf*

PART ONE

# Meet Mama

*Gladys Seedorf*

*Willie Jewel Peterson*

# Willie's Story

My mother, Willie Jewel Peterson, was born on January 17, 1935 in Greenville, Alabama. She was one of 14 children and lived on a farm with her mother, Elnora Dunklin, and father, Clate Crenshaw. Her parents were poor farmers, but they worked hard and demanded that their children worked hard as well.

Willie was not given the opportunity to go to school past the 6th grade, as her father required her help on the farm. Although she often spoke of having a very hard life, not having much money or food, there was never any sign of bitterness or resentment.

She received one new dress and a pair of shoes each year. If the shoes became too worn then her father would string them together with wire. Meals were very skimpy and usually consisted of milk, cornbread and syrup and perhaps a piece of crow, rabbit or raccoon.

After leaving home at the age of nineteen she went to Panama City, Florida, to live with an uncle who owned a small grocery store. She found work wherever she could at the local factories canning pickles, tomatoes, etc. She would later meet Louis Peterson and get married in Cambridge, Maryland. After being married a few years, she had a child that died of Pneumonia at the age of 6 months.

Willie recalls being so poor that there was barely enough money to heat the house, let alone pay for a funeral service for her dead child. This was a very difficult time in her life, as money was very scarce and jobs were few.

As time went on, her frustration grew along with a desire to have a better life. By this time she had two small children. She decided to move to Albion, Michigan, after talking to her sister, Frankiebell, who resided there. Little did she know that her sister would die shortly after her arrival.

Although her support group diminished she was determined to make a life for herself and the family. She and my father had left the South and traveled to the North, hoping and praying that they could find steady employment. My father found work at a factory, and she was hired at the local hospital as a housekeeper.

*Wedding Dress made by Willie Peterson*

In addition to her job she had a sewing business, which she ran from the basement of her home. She had a sign made, which she placed in the front yard. She was a very talented seamstress and made everything from wedding gowns to curtains, quilts, etc. My sister and I were often the best-dressed children at the church.

She and my father always had a huge garden that required a lot of hard work and effort from the family. It was mandatory that my sister and I learned how to can and preserve the vegetables.

After she retired she completed her G.E.D. at the age of 65. She understood that she was needed to work on the farm as a child, but she also longed to be educated. She once mentioned that, if she had been fortunate to receive her education, perhaps she might have tried to do something at the White House.

She wanted to purchase rental property to increase her income. She had a good mind for business and worked well with people in the community. At one time, I recall that she and my father owned four houses. She loved to work on her properties after working at the hospital.

Willie was also a member of the local church and was very active as a Sunday School Teacher, Missionary, Children's Choir Director and Usher Board President.

She was very proud of her cooking. Although money was always scarce, you could almost always find a homemade sour cream pound cake or sweet potato pie in the kitchen. Mama was simply an awesome cook. She loved to cook and bake cakes from scratch, of course. She often invited the Pastor and his wife over for dinner. She also made lots of baked goods for her doctors and neighbors. She had a reputation of being one of the best cooks in town and was often called upon to prepare dishes for church and community functions. On many occasions she was paid for her talent.

Mama's favorite part of the church service was praise and testimony. She never hesitated to belt out a song. She definitely had a Southern tenor tone, which set her apart from anybody else. She would beat her tambourine and sing like it was nobody's business. She was always ready and willing to sing and tell of the goodness of the Lord.

Obviously there weren't many vacations, due to the fact that there wasn't a lot of money. However, there was one vacation in particular that stood out in my mind. Mama called her sister, who happened to live in Washington, D.C., to inform her of our plan to visit.

Mama knew that her sister did not have a lot of money either, nor did she want to be a burden during our visit. She informed her that she would bring the food, so she need not worry. Mama called and made airline arrangements for about $50 for a round trip, at that time.

We arrived in Washington, and my aunt just happened to be dating someone that had a limousine service. We were chauffeured back to my aunt's house and all over Washington as if we were wealthy. We just thought this was the coolest thing. At dinnertime Mama opened her suitcase and pulled out a turkey that she had cooked and froze for the trip. She also pulled out a homemade pound cake and several jars of canned greens.

We were so shocked, as we had no idea that she carried such wonderful food in her suitcase. We laughed every time we ate, but we sure did enjoy the food.

I learned a valuable lesson at an early age: you don't have to spend a lot of money in order to have a good time. Mama always did the best she could with what little she had. She never made any excuses, yet she was proud that things were as well as they were.

I recall, on one occasion, I was ashamed of our family car, as it was an old Ford. She drove me to school, and I begged her to let me out approximately one block before school.

She became very angry and told me that I should be glad I had a car to ride in at all, because at least I wasn't walking. She refused to let me get out of the car before dropping me off right in front of the school. Looking back, I have no idea why I felt ashamed. None of my friends had ever mentioned or made fun of me, nor did they arrive in a better-looking vehicle than mine.

I learned another valuable lesson that day: Don't be ashamed of what you have. Instead be thankful, as things could indeed be much worse!

Part Two

# What Mama Said & Why

## *Things could always be worser than it is.*

The fact that Mama always felt that things could be worse would really upset me. I honestly felt just the opposite, and that things should be much better. I declared that she had a poor outlook on life. She was very calm, verbalized understanding and even agreed that she may be wrong. But she also suggested that I show her how to live life and a better way to think.

No sooner than I had criticized her, I immediately realized that she was actually right I recognized that I should certainly be thinking along the same lines.

# *This ol' world ain't hardly fit to live in.*

Mama always tried to see the good in everything and in everybody. Sometimes tragic events would occur, but she always thought the bad definitely outweighed the good.

## *The more you stir in the shit, the more it stinks.*

If involved in a dispute with someone, and the conversation escalates, have sense enough to shut up and go on about your business. Don't keep arguing or explaining your position.

The fact that you had the last word is NOT important. Whatever the topic, it's simply not worth losing friendship, marriage or even a life over it, according to Mama.

## *We got to pay our bills after Christmas is gone, so we can't spend a lot on presents.*

Christmastime was happy, but certainly a very plain and simple holiday at our house. We focused more on the true meaning of Christmas rather than on gifts, toys, etc. Mama was very realistic about what she could and could not afford. She was a seamstress, so she always made us a new dress and bought shoes for church. In addition, we usually got one toy. That pretty much summed up our Christmas.

*Gladys Seedorf*

## *I ain't comin' late, and I ain't leavin' late. Im only gon' work eight hours, then I'm goin' home .*

Mama had an awesome work ethic. She took very little time off, and worked whether she was sick or not; but she had no trouble letting her employer know that she had a life outside of work that needed tending to as well.

*Talk plain and don't neva' beat round the bush, 'cause somebody might not undastand you.*

Mama was a very matter of fact person. Although she wasn't educated and had quite a Southern accent, there was never any question as to what she said. Mama felt that she was good enough to talk to anybody.

*Gladys Seedorf*

# *If you think you done hurt somebody's feelings, just say you sorry and be done wit it.*

I watched Mama closely while growing up. She wouldn't hesitate to go directly to the individual or stand up in front of the church congregation and apologize if she felt she had done something wrong or hurt someone's feelings.

The fact that people carried around hurt and bad feelings was like trying to carry a large bucket of water according to Mama. She suggested that the bucket be dumped as soon as possible, so that you could move on with life.

After she apologized, she acted as if nothing had ever happened. She was also very forgiving when others apologized to her as well. She still acted as if nothing happened. She honestly didn't know how to hold a grudge.

## *You got to work hard for what you get, 'cause ain't nobody givin' nothin' away.*

Nothing is free in this world and everything costs money. We were taught to work for what we got and to not expect to be taken care of by anyone, including a boyfriend, husband or the government. At the age of sixteen, I was hired as a waitress at a restaurant. She very quickly informed me that she was no longer planning to buy me any more clothes.

*Some people just ain't gonna have nothing. Even if you give 'em something, they won't have sense enough to keep it.*

Mama thought some people were just plain old lazy, poor money managers and bad decision makers. She believed everyone should work hard, delay gratification and accomplish their goals. This is exactly how she lived her life.

## *You got to drive like you drivin on egg shells, when snow on the ground; icy roads don't know nobody.*

Mama did not like to drive on icy roads, but she did what she had to do. She was nervous, because she knew her car was subject to slide out of control. She did not want to hurt anybody, nor did she want to be the one to get hurt. She respected the winter conditions, as much as possible.

## *You betta' watch them people that talk a lot, 'cause they probly tellin' a bunch a' lies.*

Mama wasn't a big fan of people that talked a lot or even those who talked very fast. She would often watch and listen carefully, only to conclude that half of what was said was actually a lie.

# *If it's free, you sho' betta' go get it.*

Although Mama was a poor person, she neither felt bad nor ashamed, but she insisted on taking advantage of any programs or services in the community that were free such as soup kitchens. Welfare via the government was not an option for Mama, as she felt she could work 2 jobs, if necessary.

## *Now look at what you done dun, you done made me sin!*

It took an awful lot to make Mama mad. She wasn't one to cuss unless she truly felt cornered. Once in a great while, she would blurt out a word that would shock you, and you knew then that she was really mad. I always found a bit of humor in it, because she honestly felt that she had been forced into cussing.

## *If somebody don't want to be bothed wit you, just leave em lone.*

Mama thought she was just as good as anybody else. If she ran across someone that really didn't particularly care for her, she wasted no time moving on. She thought it was their loss if they chose not to take the time to get to know her or be friendly. Perhaps it may have been a blessing in disguise, according to Mama.

*Gladys Seedorf*

## *Yo chile is yo first priority, cause cherin don't ask to be born*

Once you became a mother, everything else is secondary; whether you like it or not, based on Mama's beliefs.

## *You can always find somethin wrong if that's what you lookin' for.*

Mama always saw the glass as being half full instead of half empty. She wasn't one to complain or wallow in the fact that things weren't particularly up to standard. She was also a firm believer in giving people the benefit of the doubt without passing judgment.

*Gladys Seedorf*

## *Now I done tol' y'all ova' and ova' and ova' to get in the house befo' dark. Mmm, Mmm, Mmm!*

If the streetlights came on and you weren't home, you knew you were in big trouble. Mama knew that nothing good ever happened after dark.

## *Live as long as you can, and die when you just can't help it.*

Mama believed in making the most of each day. If she was sick or had a cold, she forged ahead as if she wasn't. As a child, I remember staying home from school very few times. She believed I would feel better once I got to school and saw my friends. Most of the time, I did.

## *Treat people like you want to be treated.*

It was demanded that I treat others the way I expected to be treated. Lying, talking down to others and disrespect was absolutely not tolerated. Even when others chose to disrespect me I was told to walk away, or simply exclude those people from my social milieu.

*Chile', don't worry bout other people, 'cause they probably just jealous.*

Mama, always knew how to make you feel oh, so special. By the time she got through talking, you felt like the whole world wanted what you had. She really knew how to boost your self-esteem.

*Gladys Seedorf*

# *Don't ask to go no where on Satday, 'cause we got to clean this house up.*

Being poor was one thing, but dirty was entirely different and Mama would have no part of it. Every Saturday, we cleaned the entire house from top to bottom. We swept, mopped, dusted, scrubbed walls, washed windows, took out trash, did laundry and painted, if necessary.

When Spring-cleaning time came around, it meant nothing to us, because all chores were already done. As a child, I found it quite humorous to hear people say they were Spring-cleaning.

## *It's not a good idea for cherin' to spend the night way from home.*

Mama was no fool. She knew that some children fell prey to sexual and physical abuse. She wasn't about to have one of her children become the victim, especially during an overnight sleepover. She never explained her reasoning to us as children, but we figured things out as we grew up.

# *Right is right; wrong is wrong.*

Mama didn't hesitate to correct you if you were wrong, or support you if you were right. It didn't matter where you were or what the situation, she stood for what was right, even if she was negatively impacted.

She didn't believe young children should be disrespectful or disobedient to any authoritative figure. On the other hand, she didn't allow any adult to mistreat or disrespect me either.

Although she was uneducated and had quite a Southern accent, she would march right into the Principal's office and demand to know exactly what happened. Sometimes, she felt that I was at fault; and other times, she found fault with the teachers. By the time she left the building, all involved were on the same page.

## *If you want to get married, then you sho' betta' not move in with that man. If he already goin to bed with you, why would he want to marry you?*

*Wedding dress made by Willie Peterson*

Mama did not believe in people living together while they decided if they were compatible. She believed that young ladies should set high standards for themselves; not become sexually active until they were actually married. The fact that you weren't sure simply meant you weren't ready for marriage, and you certainly shouldn't be living in sin while you decided.

*Gladys Seedorf*

## *It don't do you no good to be interested in somebody if they ain't interested in you.*

Mama felt it improper to waste time trying to impress a man that had no intentions of keeping company with her. She made it quite clear that it was more important to consider the options available and make a choice based on the man that happened to provide the best qualifications.

## *Marriage ain't nothing but a ringer, I call it a ringer, ringer, ringer. Every time I turn aroun something else is wrong.*

Truly, Mama's marriage wasn't the best, but she tried to make the best of it indeed. My father certainly wasn't the easiest person to work with, as far as relationship issues. I commend her for holding the family together as long as she did.

Although her marriage ended in divorce, she felt that she had done everything within her power to keep peace. She continued to show kindness and compassion, after the divorce as well.

After being divorced about ten years, my father died on November 9, 2010. Mama, very willingly, paid for all the funeral arrangements. My father certainly wasn't one to carry a life insurance policy on himself or anyone else. Mama insisted that it was simply the right thing to do.

There was nothing shabby about the funeral, which would have met anyone's standards.

*Gladys Seedorf*

I thought the entire funeral service was very touching and beautiful. It's really rather sad that he never realized what a "jewel" he actually had. I grew up thinking and feeling that my father wanted something from life that just didn't exist.

*If you and yo' boyfriend go to visit yo' girlfriend, be sho' to take yo' boyfriend wit' you when you leave.*

Mama knew the possibilities of relationships. She was always one step ahead of her opponent, and she was not embarrassed about it.

*Gladys Seedorf*

# *There just ain't a lot of men out there to choose from.*

Mama strongly felt that the selection of men with good morals and values was greatly diminished. I would often sit, watch and listen to Mama pray and cry aloud. She often prayed for God to bless her children with good husbands, good jobs and good homes. God must have heard her prayers, because I think I did just fine in all three areas. If she happened to pause during a prayer and notice me sitting nearby, she would not hesitate to grab me by the hand, swing me around and demand I kneel beside her. At times, I thought fire would rain down from heaven, as a result of such intense prayers.

## *If a man leaves his wife for you, don't you know he gonna leave you for some other woman one of these days?*

Mama strongly objected to women having relationships with married men or visa versa. She felt that women should have nothing to do with taking men away from their wives or families, even if the relationship is already crumbling. She felt that such behavior was morally wrong and would only lead to destruction.

*Gladys Seedorf*

# *A man is good in his place.*

The old saying, "A woman can do whatever a man can do, only better" was something with which Mama disagreed. Mama was always tickled to have Dad around when heavy lifting needed to be done or grass mowed. Other times, she honestly felt that he should mind his own business.

## *I can't give no man all my money.*

Mama strongly felt that women should be in control of their money rather than turn it over to their husbands, even to pay bills.

She was not opposed to having a joint bank account, but she certainly felt that if a woman had the sense to go to work then she should also have the freedom to spend some or most of her money without having a discussion with her husband.

*Gladys Seedorf*

# *Don't neva give nobody yo' last dolla.*

Money was always an issue with Mama. She could make a dollar last for a year if she had to. She wasn't about to give anybody her last dollar; not even the Church.

*Chile, you ain't got to worry. If he don't want to take his medicine or go to the doctor, just put some insurance on him.*

Mama thought everyone should have insurance, in case of death or injury. She knew that her income was limited and she would need money to cover any medical or funeral expenses.

After I complained to her about my husband refusing to go to the doctor for his illness, this was her suggestion.

*Gladys Seedorf*

## *If you don't have sense enough to save yo money, when you get old, you ain't gonna have nothin to live off cept your Social Security!*

Daddy was certainly not as frugal as Mama. In fact, he was downright wasteful, at times. I would often laugh when she said these words to him, because I thought she was being too hard on him. Lo and behold! It happened just like she said. Today Daddy is retired, and all he has is his Social Security.

*A little is betta than none, and a bird in yo hand is worth more than 1,000 in the bushes. Mama was extremely prudent and insisted on making the most of every penny. She would make one dollar last until she received her next paycheck.*

She thought it was ridiculous to spend your last dollar hoping to win $10 more. Needless to say she didn't believe in gambling, raffle tickets, etc.

## *Don't neva' neva' re-mortgage your house. Leave yo' payments just like they give it to you.*

Mama was a stickler about bills, money, etc. She thought if you created a bill, then you should pay the bill just as you agreed to do. with no excuses.

She disagreed with the fact that you could re-mortgage even for lower rates, because even though your payments would be lower, they would also be lengthened, which may cause you to suffer a financial loss.

# *I'm runnin' on a rim.*

If Mama said these words, she was truly flat broke. And there was no sense in asking her for any money.

*You ain't gettin' nothin', don't ask for nothin' and if you think you got to have somethin', then you betta stay home!*

Mama's belief was that children ought to be able to accompany their parents to the store without assuming that they're automatically entitled to a treat. She made it very clear before leaving home that she had very little money to spend, but it was your choice to go along if you so desired.

*What Mama Said*

# *It ain't the money you make, it what you do wit' the money you make.*

Mama worked over thirty years as a housekeeper at the local hospital. She often reported that she never made $10.00 per hour, yet she always managed to pay her bills and save money, as well. She made every penny count.

## *Get yo' self a job, save yo' money and pay yo' bills.*

The bills were paid before any groceries were bought. She was always very responsible and paid any bill that she made. She was extremely cautious and wouldn't make any bills that she didn't think she could afford to pay. To go without was a way of life that taught us restraint and discipline, as well.

## *Ain't nobody better than you, and you ain't no better than nobody else neither.*

Black, White, rich or poor; Mama always told me that I was just as good as anybody else. Maybe we didn't have a lot of money, but she told me to be proud of who I was and thankful for what I had. She said it was important to at least act as if I felt good about myself, even though there were days that my self-esteem or confidence wasn't the highest. What a great encouragement she was.

*Gladys Seedorf*

# *It ain't nothin' but a lil' taste of money or "a piece of money".*

Whether you had a taste or a piece, it was all the same to Mama. Either way, you were pretty much flat broke. We learned to live within our means, which now that I look back, really wasn't bad. It sure did beat living off credit cards, head over heels in debt.

# *Move yo hands fast! Hurry up!*

After leaving the farm Mama found work at the factories. Her income depended upon how much piece work she got done. She canned pickles, tomatoes, and picked cotton, etc. She always insisted that I move my hands fast when I did chores around the house. We were able to accomplish a lot in a short amount of time. Today, I do the same thing at my own house with my children.

***Fix yo' plate the way you would like it, and then take half of it off. That's how much you should really eat.***

Mama always had great suggestions to lose weight. At one time she was overweight, but it didn't take long for her to drop about 50 pounds by taking her own advice. This tactic was by far the most effective for her.

*We goin' to chuch on Sunday, and you ain't goin' nowhere else.*

When I was a child, church was an all day affair. Every Sunday morning, Sunday School began at 9:00 a.m. and went until 11:30 a.m. Morning worship began promptly at 11:45 a.m. and went until 2:30 or 3:00 p.m. After Mama shook everyone's hand we went home, and she most always prepared fried chicken. Along with that, we had collard greens, corn bread, black-eyed peas, Kool-aid and a sour cream pound cake.

At 7:00 pm. we headed back to church for Young People Willing Workers (YPWW), followed by evening worship at 9:00 p.m. At approximately 10:30 to 11:00 p.m. we headed back home. Of course we made a stop back to the kitchen, in hopes of eating a left over chicken leg before going to bed.

Wednesdays and Friday night services were also of the utmost importance to Mama. Services began at 6:00 p.m. and lasted until about 9:00 p.m.

Under no circumstance were we allowed to deviate from any church scheduled service unless we were deathly ill. Mama found spiritual sustenance in God, which kept her grounded and focused.

She was bound and determined that we were going to develop a relationship with God by becoming avid readers of the Bible and praying regularly. Any and everything else was secondary, according to Mama.

# *God don't love ugly*

Malevolent behaviors were deemed by Mama as ugly and could no way be justified by God, in her opinion.

*Gladys Seedorf*

# *God don't neva tell you nothin bad and that old devil don't neva tell you nothin good.*

I recall asking mama how she determined whether God or the devil was speaking to her. She gave me a very simple, but honest response. I never forgot those words that so strongly resonate in my heart and thoughts today. I know from experience that one's thoughts whether positive or negative certainly affect every aspect of their life. Although it's sometimes easier said than done I try to dwell on the positives and know that God is speaking to me.

# *Y'all get somewhere and sit down. Don't you know the Lawd is workin'?*

If it was thundering and lightning, Mama insisted that the Lord was working and we should sit quietly until the storm passed. She felt that we needed to recognize and respect the mighty roll of thunder and the power of the Lord.

## *Some of these church people is gonna bust hell wide open.*

Just because you attended church did not mean you were living a good Christian life, according to Mama. She was appalled by some of the things that the members would say and do, not only outside the church, but inside as well.

*Lawd, take us over the highways safely and bring us back.*

Mama believed you should never travel over the highways unless you ask the Lord to go with you. She frequently sang a song in church, "Take the Lord Long With You Everywhere You Go." She lived by these words.

*Gladys Seedorf*

## *Is you plannin on goin to heaven?... Well then you know you gotta forgive me.*

Mama didn't believe in holding a grudge against anyone, nor did she feel that anyone else should either if they claimed to be Christians and loved GOD. She insisted that you were fooling yourself if you planned on going to heaven, but yet couldn't forgive your neighbor. To forgive is not a choice, but a commandment according to mama. She lived by the rule that sincere apologies should be made by both and then move on as if nothing every happened.

## *You got to live like you little.*

Mama believed that you should live life and use whatever resources or talents, with which God blessed you, in order to help other people. She was very impressed by people that she knew were wealthy, yet who were living very humble, quiet lives.

*Gladys Seedorf*

## *Always read yo Bible for yoself, 'cause some of these preachers ain't no good.*

Although Mama wasn't the greatest reader, she knew the Bible pretty well. She wasn't about to let some preacher lead her down the wrong path. She felt that God was no respecter of persons and would speak to her just as He spoke to the preachers.

## *You gonna reap what you sow.*

Regardless of your actions, whether good or bad, Mama let you know you would be repaid by God. Mama highly recommended that time be spent on good actions only.

*Gladys Seedorf*

# *If it's the Lawd's will.*

Mama was a very devout Christian. Perhaps it was natural to trust in the Good Lord, especially since she grew up dirt poor and worked hard for every morsel. No plans or promises were ever made without the prefix, "If it's the Lord's will."

## *Everything down here belongs to God, so we might as well use it.*

God created heaven and earth, and since we're just passing through, Mama believed we should use what we needed. She refused to believe that anything was too good for us. Now we certainly weren't able to afford much of anything, but if for some strong reason we could, then that was fine with Mama.

*Gladys Seedorf*

PART THREE

# Mama's Favorite Songs & Scripture

*Gladys Seedorf*

# This Little Light of Mine

This little light of mine
I'm gonna let it shine.
Oh, this little light of mine
I'm gonna let it shine.
Oh, this little light of mine
I'm gonna let it shine.

Let it shine. Let it shine. Let it shine.

All in my home
I'm gonna let it shine.
Oh, all in my home
I'm gonna let it shine.
Oh, all in my home
I'm gonna let it shine.

Let it shine. Let it shine. Let it shine.
My Lawd give it to me
Told me to let it shine.
My Lawd give it to me
Told me to let it shine.
Oh, my Lawd give it to me
Told me to let it shine.

Let it shine. Let it shine. Let it shine.

# 99 and a 1/2 Won't Do

Lawd, I'm runnin
Tryin to make 100.
99 and a 1/2 won't do.
Lawd, I'm runnin
Trying to make 100.
99 and a 1/2 won't do.

It won't do, Lawd
It won't do.
99 and a ½ won't do.
It won't do, Lawd.
It won't do.
99 and a ½ won't do.

Lawd, I'm prayin
Tryin to make 100.
99 and a 1/2 won't do.
Lawd, I'm prayin
Trying to make 100.
99 and a 1/2 won't do.

It won't do, Lawd
It won't do.
99 and a ½ won't do.
It won't do, Lawd.
It won't do.
99 and a ½ won't do.

*Gladys Seedorf*

# Travlin Shoes

travlin shoes, Lawd
Got on my travlin shoes
travlin shoes, Lawd
Got on my travlin shoes
I can travel now
travlin shoes, Lawd
Got on my travlin shoes

# I Know It Was the Blood

I know it was the blood
I know it was the blood for me
One Day when I was lost
He died upon the cross
I know it was the blood for me

*Gladys Seedorf*

# I Don't Know What I Would Do Without the Lawd

I don't know what I'd do without the Lawd.
I don't know what I'd do without the Lawd.

As I look around to see
what the Lawd has done for me.
I don't know what I'd do without the Lawd.

He has kept me from all evil
With a mind stayed on Him
I don't know what I'd do without the Lawd.

# Proverbs 31:10-31

New International Version (NIV)
Epilogue: The Wife of Noble Character

[10] A wife of noble character who can find?
She is worth far more than rubies.
[11] Her husband has full confidence in her
and lacks nothing of value.
[12] She brings him good, not harm,
all the days of her life.
[13] She selects wool and flax
and works with eager hands.
[14] She is like the merchant ships,
bringing her food from afar.
[15] She gets up while it is still night;
she provides food for her family
and portions for her female servants.
[16] She considers a field and buys it;
out of her earnings she plants a vineyard.
[17] She sets about her work vigorously;
her arms are strong for her tasks.
[18] She sees that her trading is profitable,
and her lamp does not go out at night.
[19] In her hand she holds the distaff
and grasps the spindle with her fingers.
[20] She opens her arms to the poor
and extends her hands to the needy.
[21] When it snows, she has no fear for her household;

for all of them are clothed in scarlet.
$^{22}$ She makes coverings for her bed;
she is clothed in fine linen and purple.
$^{23}$ Her husband is respected at the city gate,
where he takes his seat among the elders of the land.
$^{24}$ She makes linen garments and sells them,
and supplies the merchants with sashes.
$^{25}$ She is clothed with strength and dignity;
she can laugh at the days to come.
$^{26}$ She speaks with wisdom,
and faithful instruction is on her tongue.
$^{27}$ She watches over the affairs of her household
and does not eat the bread of idleness.
$^{28}$ Her children arise and call her blessed;
her husband also, and he praises her:
$^{29}$ "Many women do noble things,
but you surpass them all."
$^{30}$ Charm is deceptive, and beauty is fleeting;
but a woman who fears the LORD is to be praised.
$^{31}$ Honor her for all that her hands have done,
and let her works bring her praise at the city gate.

PART FOUR

# Mama's Favorite Recipes

*Gladys Seedorf*

# Baked Sweet Potatoes

3 lbs sweet potatoes
½ cup maple syrup or dietetic syrup
½ cup packed brown sugar
2 T butter
½ t salt
1 t nutmeg

Cook potatoes in boiling water until tender, 30-40 minutes; drain; peel. Cut sweet potatoes into 1 inch slices. In a saucepan combine maple syrup, brown sugar, butter, salt and nutmeg. Bring to a boil; then simmer 5 minutes. Place pots in an 11.75 x 1.5 inch baking pan. Spoon syrup over potatoes to coat. Bake uncovered at 350° for 30 minutes, basting potatoes frequently. Makes 8-10 servings.

# Red Velvet Cake

2 ½ cups flour
1 ½ cups sugar
1 t baking soda
1 t cocoa
1 cup buttermilk
1 cup butter flavor Wesson oil
½ cup regular Wesson oil
1 t vinegar
2 eggs
1 bottle red food coloring
1 t vanilla

Gently mix all ingredients, and pour into 2 round cake pans. Cook at 350° for 25 minutes.

*Gladys Seedorf*

## *Frosting*

1 stick margarine/butter
8 oz package cream cheese
1 box powdered sugar
½ t vanilla

Gently mix all ingredients together

# Sweet Potato Pie

1 t nutmeg
3 eggs
3 cups sugar
1 t vanilla
½ cup flour
¾ - 1 cup milk
½ cup butter
2 ½ cups sweet potatoes

Gently mix all ingredients, and pour into 2 regular pie crusts. Let them cook approx. 1 to 1 ½ hours. When they turn slightly brown take them out.

*Gladys Seedorf*

# Sour Cream Pound Cake

3 cups sifted flour
2 ¾ cups sugar
1 cup sour cream
1 t salt
1 t vanilla extract
½ t baking soda
1 cup butter or margarine
6 eggs

Gently mix ingredients, and bake at 350° for approx. 1 hour and 10 minutes.

# Ice Box Rolls

2 yeast cakes (50% faster rise)
½ cup sugar
2 t salt
2 T shortening
2 cups hot water
2 eggs
7 cups flour (sifted)


Dissolve 2 yeast cakes in ½ cup warm water. Put ½ cup sugar, 2 teaspoons salt, 2 tablespoons (heaping) shortening in large bowl. Mix. Pour in 2 cups hot water. Beat 2 eggs and add to yeast and mix. Add 7 cups sifted flour. Mix; do not knead.

*Gladys Seedorf*

This makes a very soft dough. Grease hands well when making out rolls. Let stand for one hour or until it doubles its size. Make out rolls and let rise another hour. Grease pan before putting in pan. Bake in 400° oven until golden brown.

# Hummingbird Cake

3 cups all-purpose flour
2 cups sugar
1 t baking soda
1 t ground cinnamon
3 eggs
1 cup vegetable oil
1 t vanilla
1 8 ounce can crushed pineapple (undrained)
2 cups sliced bananas
2 cups chopped pecans

## *Frosting*

2 pkgs Philadelphia Cream Cheese
2 sticks of butter
2 16 ounce boxes Confectioner's Sugar
2 t vanilla

Mix dry ingredients, and stir in remaining ingredients. Use 3 greased cake pans. Bake at 300° for 25 minutes. Mix together ingredients for frosting. Sprinkle pecans on top.

# In Conclusion.......

**Willie** currently resides in Albion, Michigan. Although her health has declined, she still lives independently. During the summer she plants a big garden and enjoys lots of fresh vegetables. In the winter months, she loves to haul in lots of wood to burn in her fireplace. Willie attends church regularly and occasionally volunteers with the Red Cross. She continues to bless

*Gladys Seedorf*

others through her words of wisdom and acts of kindness.

# About the Author

**Gladys J. Seedorf** was born in Cambridge, Maryland and raised in Albion, Michigan.

After graduating from Western Michigan University Gladys earned a Masters degree in Social Work. She has worked in Hospitals, Hospice, and Homecare agencies for the past twenty years providing services to homebound senior citizens.

Gladys lives with her husband and two daughters in Battle Creek, Michigan. This is her first book.